SEALED

INNA KRASNOPER

Published by Black Sunflowers Poetry Press
www.blacksunflowerspoetry.com

© Inna Krasnoper 2024

ISBN: 978-1-7396267-8-5

All rights reserved

CONTENTS

"i mistook my doctor for somebody else…" 1
"will you remarry me marry..." 3
"i'm in a hurry to harvard..." 4
"unknown people know nothing of me..." 5
"as i talk to you, i miss calling your name..." 7
"how long is the letter i…" 9
"there is this liking…" 10
"i got into a poem once or twice – you know…" 11
"look at me / what you see…" 13
"Not that you were not there and not…" 14
"maybe i am here to call things by their name…" 15
"what has it to do with me…" 17
"did you touch my english…" 19
"it isn't my concert my concern my act..." 20
"have you seen a noun?…" 21
"j'arrive à paris lundi..." 22
"i am a russian with many cats..." 24
"excuse my french..." 25
"here is the origin of my poem..." 27
"i do not have a word for you..." 29

Acknowledgements 31

*
i mistook my doctor for somebody else
i took a doctor for an appointment

i appointed my doctor to be somebody else
i forgot what i mistook my doctor for

i forgot how forgetful a doctor could be
i reconsidered myself and asked for a doctor

i doctored myself, before going for a master's
i rediscovered how good an appointment could be

i appointed myself to forget
i appointed myself to forget how to call a doctor

i appointed them to call for a doctor
i appointed them to forget

i forgot, i could call for a doctor
i have forgotten, i could have called for one

for one or another reason, an appointment has been forgotten
for better or worse, there has been an appointment

for no reason sunday is today

for a good reason, someone could have been appointed
but someone wasn't

not one of my appointments comes today
on one of my appointments i called for a doctor
loudly

having had no appointments recently, i called myself
to remember

an appointment calls for the act of appointing

appointing today to be sunday, we could stay weak

if this were a country where sunday was a weekday
we could call for an appointment

but then, if this were also a holy day
no appointments could have been made

*

will you remarry me marry
will you remember me marry
will you remarry me member
will you be my memory member

will you remarry me marta
will you refrain from sharing this franny
will you repost about my marriage marta
will you regain *morte*   *death*

will you have some energy tomorrow martin
will you give some reassurance martin
are you sure to tell this to shura
are you sharing my nightmare martin

is tomorrow a *matin*   *morning*
is tomorrow a *maintenant*   *now*

завтра завтрак   *tomorrow breakfast*
morgen morgen   *morning tomorrow*

when will they come for maintenance
saturday morning, dear tenant

*
i'm in a hurry to harvard
i'm in a harvard to hurry
i'm harry when not howard
i'm howwe

how are we harvesting harry
how hairy is howard
hey is it howard who is so hairy
is he approaching his harvest
horrendous is what this harry is

i am less red than harry
i have nowhere to hurry

if i did have a harry to hurry to
i would have to take my hair into account

for hair takes a lot of weight and space
all the way around

i like berries from time to time
sometimes a berry is also hairy

sometimes it is bald
i would not live until going

who knows what i would live up to
anticipating some hurrying to do

*

unknown people know nothing of me
none of the unknown people know to know

me. embracing the air
of unknown people – we get to hug

people we don't know
that they are there

over the shoulder – we get to see
hey there, do i know you

do i un-know you
while embracing the air

i breathe into the air – of unknown people
and then, pull something back

another part of the air
which part of the year
yet unknown

i know the people that i know
they are round around me

just like the word "know"
acknowledge that

stubborn word
against knowing

hey people, do we get to know each other
do we other each other. do you acknowledge

my presence in front of you
i am round. i am a people

i peep around. around you and other yous
i surround you

with effort and attention
affording to un-know you

i now you
i un-noun you

with yous. i you
no?

*

as i talk to you, i miss calling your name
i miss saying your name, before

i say hi. i say privet
as if i am about to touch

on a matter. to call you by "you"
a name creates certain distance

probably a fair dis tance
like between stanzas or in tanz

with tanz it's fair to be at a distance

though to measure the distance not visually
but sensually, to sense the space in between

while writing i have the urge to separate

from what i just said
and yet: i don't like to call

you by name. it means
to take a step further

away. further
from what? i prefer

when there's only one
possible name

unless you are so close as
to come up with any name

or the name your mother might call you
and yet i'm all for distance

even cold and indifferent
as long as there is a difference

between any one and any other
to depart from, to leave

some one *or* some other
in the other stanza

and let myself hang
in between no-betweens

*
how long is the letter i
how lonely is the letter i
how long is the sound you
how deep is the sound
how deep is the sea
have you seen the letter i
did it show up
did it show down
how long is the downtime of
a downing letter i
of a drowning letter
of a drawn letter
of a gesture of letter to the left
of a left letter
to stay
unattended
unended
in a long sounding ungestured
letter
in a let be letter
in a let it litter
in a letter trying to
tail lettre
in pursuing the latter
in catching the letter
at its end

having consulted with a
tailor

```
_ _/////~`/\\\~~~_
~`{{{{\\\V//`'///
   _ _''꜔꜔꜔꜔- --{{{-`[[
```

there is this liking

What is this gesture
it is the knowing

How is the knowing
{it does} Like liking

Like linking. Like rounding
Like male-ing. Like stealing

like stalking, like standing

Like weaving

*

i got into a poem once or twice – you know
and then i didn't

and then i got into a poem by someone else
and then i didn't

and then i thought i did, but i actually didn't – it was
someone else, you know

and then i got other people into my poems
i dragged them in

and then they didn't fit inside my poem
their legs or other body parts were taking them out

they couldn't stay inside a poem – for too long
also, you know, lvovsky writes:

i don't write about real people
это я пишу о тех   *i am writing this about those*
кто живёт внутри меня   *who live inside me*
а не о них самих – he says, to be exact   *not about them as they are*

so whose legs were those, sticking
out of my poems

and did any of my legs or other extremities
get into any of your poems

skirts, you say
well

all my skirts are accounted for
they are right here

right here in the middle
of dropping

from [an inky dropping:
splat splat]

a poem

*

look at me / what you see
look at you / what you see

look at you / what see you
look at you / see you what

what do you see when you look at
at what look you when / see you

see you when you look at / see
see you look at when it sees / you

you have lost what you look / see
at look what has seen / you

at the same / look has seen
you
lost have that look / see

who has seen you at look
last

looking you / have seen that
of the look

of the look / look seen you
every time

every time you have been
that of look

giving time / of that look
seeing you / seen it lock
have you then / at the time

time that look / seen has that
that of look

*

Not that you were not there and not
Not that you were not there and not yet
Not yet were you there and yet it went there and also

Not that you could have seen there before

Not that it might have been there and again
Not after it's been there it went

Not that it went and yet not yet
Not how it went there and then again

While

Not after it has been almost
at last

Not that it came moving along

Not like this has been in a scene and yet *sinnvoll*　　　　　*sensible*
Not how it came like it went

Not after and not during

But then

No pathway and no *взрослый*　　　　　*grownup*
and hey

*

maybe i am here to call things by their name
maybe i am here to call out simple direct things

maybe i am here to deny the wish to hide
maybe i am just here

maybe i am here to freeze

maybe i am here to freeze the way that doesn't silence
maybe i am here to pick the slice of uncertainty

maybe i am here not for you
maybe i am here not for the idea of a nice woman

maybe i am here not to support the idea of another nice woman
maybe i am here to acknowledge

maybe i am here not to acknowledge
the presence of a nice young woman

maybe i am not here for you
maybe i am here for being here

maybe i am here to call things by their name
and stop the magic

maybe the magic you reference is disturbing
maybe the magic you or anyone references in their fairytales
is deeply disturbing

maybe this magic is deeply discriminating
maybe it is – right now – denying someone the right to be

maybe someone gave up without knowing it
not realizing she is not here anymore

try hard, and harder still – until she is not here
until you can observe the physical damage

until the physical damage is very physical
and cannot be restored

how would you know
you are busy with your magic

how would you know
you are busy

*
what has it to do with me
what has it done to me
what has it me
no me   has it done to me
no done   has it to consider to me
no cider have i been drinking
recently
no scent has my *трусы* to distribute   *panties*
no tribute to what it has done to me

no done in   as far as one could see
no attribution ending the word
no word   to attribute to
no biting   as far as one could reach
no reaching across

the word is a sounding in multitude
it sounds as far as one could hear

ROAR is a word
it is a word to be roared
to be con-firmed
a firm word

in a family of words roar is quite raw
at the same time, one needs to roar affirmably
in order to be roared
the road leads to a sound that has potential
a sound is potentially raw
it is cooked in sounding
in ending multiply
additionally, what a st-ory
orally the story is to be told
in forking directions we multiply the story
and then it writes
it covers letters with sound
and back

uncovers the sound in letters

in letters that are written
rites of sense to sense right
to detect

we spring upon rites
our rites of spring

is this right?
why does "rite" sound like *луч* to me   *ray of light*
i wouldn't know

let's let it be луч
rite could be луч
and *по лучше* than no луч   *no better*

if it is not a луч
it would sound to me like one

one of the beams would be луч
and another one – rite

let me be right about this
at least in one thing
i could be right

i could sound like this
in search of the right word
for what i'm saying

*

did you touch my english
did you detach my english
did you debrief my english
did you break my english
did you english with my english
did you fool around with my english
did you ask my english for favors
did you depart from my favor
in a boat

were you giving it the cold shoulder
how do you like my english
have you listened to it
did you pay attention
did you pay it a visit
have you visited my england

have you been landing around here
are you attached to my english
would you retouch my english
would you give it a dressing down
have you passed by my english
have you entered the field of my english
what flowers grow there
have you walked around my english
were you on an *eng* leash   *tight*
did you pass up on my english
would you pass my english on
does my english leave you at an impasse
would you turn the other way
would you listen with another ear
has my ear been long enough for you
does this belong in english
does this belong in english

did you include something that doesn't belong here

   *
   it isn't my concert my concern my act
i am not the one that is acting
   it's not being acted upon or contracted
   under the weather
i am not getting under it
   getting down or about
i am not talking about it
i am not it, and it – isn't to be expected
i am not electing to hear this
i am not hearing it, and it – will not be heard
   it will not take place
   be held or cradled
i am not a crocodile, cracker or anything except for polly
i will not polish this, it's not gonna get polished
   brushed or waxed over
i will not get vexed about the time
   and effort of getting ready to go
     o u t
   out of here i did not learn how to finish
   nor will i accomplish it
   at close range

*
have you seen a noun?
it's in town
it's a-noun-ing every side of the town
it's a-town-ing – announcing the town
it is pronouncing that the town is a town
atop of the town – *топчутся люди*   *there are people milling about*
tapping on the town, making it more towny
a typical town with some typos
the type of a noun to stum-ble upon
and go down uptown
on top of that, is a town also the place of a swamp
if you want to swim around, come visit
a liquidy town
liquidating all the angles about town
the town could at least have some pumps
a town can't have too many stumps
but on the other hand
a stump was once a tree
at least this poem will not be getting into print
its noun and no-noun are not remarkable
it will not mark a town with its print
it might walk around, leaving some trace
a trace of a _ _ _ _ to be left alone
"let us think on a clear day
sitting down on stump and stone"[1]

---

[1] *From Alexander Vvedensky's "An Invitation for Me to Think," translated by Matvei Yankelevich.*

*

j'arrive à paris lundi　　　　　*on monday arriving in paris*
déjà arrivé　　　　　　　　　 *already arriving*
я уже arrivé　　　　　　　　　 *i arrived*
я уже со-жрала　　　　　　　 *con-sumed it all with passion*
со-жалела　　　　　　　　　　 *con-sternation*
со-пере-живание　　　　　　　 *com-passion*
в со-труд-ничестве　　　　　　 *in col-labor-ation*

вот мой пруф　　　　　　　　　*here is my proof*
du bist aufgerufen　　　　　　 *you are called*
du bist nicht aufgerufen　　　　 *you are not called*
please open your pass-port

wave it
way it in
please talk on your language
j'arrive
please talk
people are concerned

that your tongue is not eaten
or lost on the way

your language is as mono
as that of any citizen
it is one language
no piece is to be taken from it

no particulars
within borders
one language one destiny

what did you imagine
you'd manage?!

bite it
no piece

chew it all
don't swallow

all of it can be taken
by any other monocitizen

*

i am a russian with many cats
i'm in a rush to see my stats

i'm in a rush to hide from eyes
i have just eaten multiple pies

i have just lost the taste in mouth
especially when it comes

to coffee, ketchup, macaroni
proceed with caution

stay awa$^{y}/_{ke}$

*
excuse my french
excuse my pronunciation
excuse my nuances
excuse my notion
excuse my *ношение*   *carrying*
my *карман*   *pocket*
excuse my package
only full package
take it or leave it
no more for today
they get snapped up very quickly
excuse my capacity
don't excuse my city
it is fully to blame
excuse my fields
my gaps
don't mind my presence
excuse my essence
my sense of
my nonsense
excuse my articulation
my circulation
you got the wrong gal
excuse my *упал*   *fell*
свалился завалялся   *collapsed remained*
excuse my supplies my compasses
excuse my direction my imagery my sideways
excuse my luggage my suitcase
to get a handle on
excuse my steps my desires my tires my fatigue
excuse, *но не прощай*   *but don't forgive*
no walking without saying goodbye
excuse my conclusion my erasure my tool
take a stool, sit
that's enough – now, stand
widersteht! in a good state   *resist*

excuse my thingness my physicality my emptiness
excuse my vessel my destiny
a tiny bit
excuse my list, round up
excuse my leaning lingering lingerie
excuse my ups my downs in-betweens
excuse my twists wrists recordings
excuse my register my gestures my talk
excuse leaves and leaf
прилив *tide*
excuse my longing my lounging my propeller
point fingers lay eyes on water
translate your sentence
into this utterance

*

here is the origin of my poem
it originates from that place
it is being developed from
it derives declares devastates
it is deprived

the origin i departed from is vast
and private

i am not part of that origin anymore
nor can i know if it stays there
if it stayed once i left

an origin is enclosed
it is being enfolded
enveloped

it is being sent to another destination
it is to reach someone else
who would originate from it

an origin isn't a wind
nor can it be borne away on the wind
an origin isn't romantic
it can be a romance
it cannot be a song

it needs corporality
nearing an object but not becoming one

an origin has to be coming and moving
it is being restored, so to say, re(porting to a)store

an origin is stamping on top
it is hanging and turning
making small jumps

missing the point
misleading to a trap

wrapping around, trembling lightly
saying clearly
that you came from there

but not welcome anymore
as neither you nor there are the same

and as a matter of fact
this matter is not of a rigid form

sich festzulegen   *to settle*
fest to lie
the faster to fester

we are to declare
no clarity
in the declaration

unfastened
an origin is no engine

to shed light on

*

i do not have a word for you
my word is broken
i do not have an explanation
i keep holding to a drifting plane
i do not have a have
i cannot have anything
i cannot offer to reflect on my identity
we'll keep coming to a backdrop
i cannot proceed with a project
it's being pre-projected
i can offer a wall, a shelter
i can offer it all
as long as time keeps dropping
drop me a line
i'll keep my hand open
drop me a reflex
it'll stay sealed

Acknowledgements

Earlier versions of some poems in this chapbook appeared in *Bridge Poetry Berlin*, *Dvoetochie*, *Ghost Proposal* (featured on *Poetry Daily*), *Pocket Samovar*, *Wild Roof,* and *Alchemy.* Some of them are also included in the chapbook *Over Sight* published by Eulalia Books.

www.blacksunflowerspoetry.com

www.ingramcontent.com/pod-product-compliance
Lightning Source LLC
Chambersburg PA
CBHW061752070526
44585CB00025B/2868